~ *Craft Ideas for Your Home* ~

TRIMS AND TASSELS

~Craft Ideas for Your Home~

TRIMS AND TASSELS

VICTORIA WALLER

FRIEDMAN/FAIRFAX
PUBLISHERS

To the memory of Jerry Fried,
whose imagination and support have guided my life and career,
helping me to achieve that which I thought impossible,
and whose brilliance will continue to shine through the eyes
of those he touched.

A FRIEDMAN/FAIRFAX BOOK
© 1996 by Michael Friedman Publishing Group, Inc.

Library of Congress Cataloging-in-Publication Data available upon request

ISBN 1-56799-279-X

Editor: Elizabeth Viscott Sullivan
Art Director: Lynne Yeamans
Layout: Robbi Oppermann Firestone
Photography Editor: Colleen Branigan
Production Associate: Camille Lee
Illustrator: Barbara Hennig

Color separations by Fine Arts Repro House Co., Ltd.
Printed in China by Leefung-Asco Printers Ltd.

For bulk purchases and special sales, please contact:
Friedman/Fairfax Publishers
Attention: Sales Department
15 West 26th Street
New York, NY 10010
212/685-6610   FAX 212/685-1307

Contents

~

Introduction

At one time, luxurious decorative trimmings such as these adorned only castles and courtly European homes, representing the wealth and status of royalty. The intensive hand labor and skill required to produce passementerie created a product far too expensive for the average consumer. But the marriage of centuries-old craft with modern technology has increased the availability and affordability of these elegant trimmings. Today, craftspeople in the United States and Europe operate huge looms to pull a rainbow of cotton, rayon, silk, acrylic, and wool yarns through hundreds of needles. The needles stitch and weave while mechanical fingers take the yarn through a metamorphosis, creating a confection of color and beauty—the exquisite trimmings we find available today.

There is nothing so inviting as a beautifully decorated room resplendent in the luscious colors and textures of opulent trimmings such as lush, multilayered tassels, soft, silky fringes, exquisite cords, and richly textured jacquard braids embellishing pillows, upholstery, and window treatments. These decorative trims, also known as passementerie, are enjoying a resurgence in popularity worldwide. Their textures invite the touch, and impart a sense of comfort and warmth to an environment.

~

Opposite: Red is a color that usually demands attention. Here, however, it is subdued by the mocha fringes on these sofa pillows. Bullion fringe, echoing the colors of the window shade fabric, softly weights the base of the sofa as well as effectively draws the eye to the beautifully crafted balloon shade above. A shade constructed with such voluminous dark fabric could be overwhelming without the delicate tassel-fringed hem, which scales down the proportion and brings the room into perfect harmony.

~

Left: Tassels of every size, shape, and color manifest dignity, charm, and sometimes whimsy, imparting instant style upon their host. How to choose from the myriad of styles available? Details such as smaller layered tassels or loops and wraps of twisted coloration give each tassel a distinct personality and will render one style the perfect choice for a project.

You will find trims and tassels in a wide variety of styles and colors at your local fabric or craft store. Simple tailored edgings or elegantly draped fringes will add distinctive detail to traditional or formal decor. Lavish tassels combined with layered trims can impart an eclectic or exotic feel or add a splash of whimsy. You no longer have to settle for expensive prepackaged decorative accessories with minimal design and boring color palettes. Instead, you can choose your own style, fabric, and decorative trims to create one-of-a-kind finished decor at half the cost of ready-made treatments.

The following step-by-step instructions or commercial sewing patterns can be used to create stunning designer room treatments such as those shown here. If the idea of redecorating an entire room is overwhelming, create just one beautifully trimmed item to add new life to your decor. If you'd prefer not to sew, you can enhance pillows, lampshades, or covered boxes by simply gluing or tying on trims.

Occasionally, in order to match an unusual color or to create an unavailable tassel length, you may wish to make your own trimmings. Rayon fringes and cords purchased in a natural color can be easily dyed by following the instructions on dye packages. (Always experiment with a test scrap first.) Handmade tassels will give you the custom look you desire and save you a considerable amount of money, especially in the construction of large, elaborate tieback tassels. You can also layer trims of different colors to create the illusion of custom-made trimmings.

On the pages that follow you will find basic guidelines for working with passementerie. But don't hesitate to experiment with your own ideas. Who knows? You may discover a new and wonderful application for decorative trim!

Equipment and Materials

For the projects here, you will need a sewing machine, thread, hand-sewing needles, pins, a seam ripper, a tape measure, a straightedge ruler or yardstick, fabric marking pens, scissors, iron-on adhesives, and a hot-glue gun.

Sewing Machine A basic zigzag sewing machine is all that is required. Purchase machine needles size 80(12) for light- to medium-weight fabrics and 90(14)–100(16) for upholstery-weight fabrics and decorative trims. A zipper foot, included with most sewing machines, is invaluable when applying decorative trims. This foot is adjustable and allows you to stitch close to the cord or fringe. Your machine may have a seam guide to help you sew a straight line, or you can

place a piece of masking tape ½" to the right of the needle. Align the raw edge of the fabric with the masking tape as you sew for perfect ½" seams.

Thread Types   Simple sewing with decorative trimming requires no special thread, but 100 percent polyester or mercerized-cotton-covered polyester sewing thread, available in most sewing and craft stores, gives the most satisfying results. A more heavy-duty thread able to withstand the constant abuse of abrasion, stress, and environmental changes may be required in the case of upholstered furniture or outdoor cushions; nylon upholstery thread is designed especially for such projects. Before using heavier thread, test sew on a scrap of fabric first with a size 100(16)−110(18) machine needle; the machine thread tension may need to be adjusted to the best stitch. Refer to the machine manual for adjustment instructions.

Hand-Sewing Needles   Keep a package of embroidery or crewel needles in assorted sizes handy for basting or finishing throw pillows. These needles have large eyes for easy threading.

Pins   Straight pins are used to hold fabric pieces together until they are sewn. Long quilting pins with plastic or glass-ball heads are best for bulky fabrics or for attaching trims when a smaller pin might get lost. A magnetic pin holder makes cleaning up annoying pin spills a snap.

Seam Ripper   To rip out incorrect stitching or to open up a pillow casing, a seam ripper is a useful tool.

Tape Measure and Straight-edge Ruler   A tape measure is essential for planning fabric projects. One that has markings on both sides is best. A straightedge ruler or yardstick is helpful when estimating positions of window treatments or for marking straight lines; an L-shaped ruler aids in marking and cutting square corners.

Fabric Marking Pens   Fabric marking pens allow you to mark cutting lines, and starting and stopping points for sewing. Some pens are formulated to disappear with water or to evaporate after a period of time. Always test on a scrap to make sure that no marks are permanently visible on your project.

Scissors   Keep two pairs of scissors on hand: large, bent-handled shears are used for all the fabric and trim cutting; smaller embroidery scissors are perfect for clipping threads. Never use sewing scissors to cut paper or to do other household chores.

Iron-On Adhesives   These are available in 17"−18" widths or in narrow ⅜"−⅞" strips. Follow package directions for use. Be sure that the care instructions of the adhesive are compatible with the fabric or trim being used.

Hot-Glue Gun and Glue Sticks   Use to assemble tassels; also to adhere fabric or trims to cornices, lampshades, and other projects when sewing or iron-on adhesives are not practical. Never leave a plugged-in gun unattended.

Trims

Decorative trims are surprisingly easy to work with. Although various trim styles may appear to be very different, they use the same basic sewing techniques. To begin, all you will need are a sewing machine with a zipper foot and the ability to sew a straight seam. The step-by-step illustrated instructions that follow will enable you to combine basic sewing skills with several special techniques for instant success. As you experiment with variations on the basics you will soon gain the skill and confidence to tackle even the most intimidating decorative effort.

The many types of trimming have been categorized in the table "Working with Decorative Trims" (pages 10–12). As you will notice, the same tools and techniques are used for most of the trims. While you may wish to handle them differently (gluing or bonding, for example), the techniques featured in the tables that follow are the recommended methods.

First, choose the trim you wish to use. If you are unsure of the name of the trim you have in mind, refer to the descriptions in the second column. Before you begin to sew, read the other columns for tools, sewing and finishing techniques, and other tips. When working with any trim for the first time, it is a good idea to purchase an additional ⅛ yard for practice. Sew slowly at first until you feel comfortable with the technique. Don't be afraid to rip out a few stitches and start again. Patience is the one ingredient not listed in the table.

9

Working with Decorative Trims

Trim Type	Description	Size	Tools Required	Corner Sewing	Finishing	Tips
Twisted Cord	A twisted trim consisting of 2–3 sets of yarns (plies) twisted together.	Diameter: ⅛", ³⁄₁₆", ⅜", ½"	Embroidery foot or cording foot (or hand stitch)	Topical application (A); knot or loop at corners.	Overlap cord into seam allowance (B). Tuck ends under a knot or hide in a seam.	Wrap cord with tape before cutting (C); cut through tape to prevent raveling.

A **B** Overlap cord into seam allowance to finish **C** Wrap with tape before cutting

Trim Type	Description	Size	Tools Required	Corner Sewing	Finishing	Tips
Cord-Edge (Cord with a lip)	A twisted cord with an attached seam allowance for seam insertion. The seam allowance, or gimp edge, is attached with a chain stitch. Cord-edge is used to edge pillows, cushions, upholstery, cornices.	Diameter: ³⁄₁₆", ⅜", ½"	Zipper foot	Stitch along innermost row of permanent stitching. Stop stitching 1" before corner. Clip at corner; stitch to corner; pivot with needle in fabric. Push corner trim away from you; lower foot and continue stitching.	Overlap ends into seam allowance (D); or start and finish with 3" tails. Clip and remove the chain stitch connecting cord to gimp in tail only. Overlap tails, aligning cord twists; flatten cord in seam allowance; stitch over cord joint (E).	Handle cut cord ends as little as possible when retwisting cord ends to finish.

D Overlap to finish or retwist as shown in E **E** Ladderlike connecting stitches

Working with Decorative Trims

Trim Type	Description	Size	Tools Required	Corner Sewing	Finishing	Tips
Brush Fringe or Moss Fringe	A fringe that has one set of cut ends and one set of permanently stitched loops. The permanently stitched edge is inserted in a seam. Used on pillow edges, cushions, upholstery.	Length: 1"–4"	Zipper foot	See cord-edge corner sewing (page 10).	Butt ends; do not overlap (F).	Remove temporary chain stitching on cut ends after project is complete.

F

Clip corners

↑ Butt ends together to finish

Trim Type	Description	Size	Tools Required	Corner Sewing	Finishing	Tips
Loop Fringe	A fringe looped on both ends. One end is permanently stitched for insertion. Used for pillows, lampshades.	Length: 1" or longer	Zipper foot	See cord-edge corner sewing (page 10).	Butt ends; do not overlap (F).	Ravels easily; stitch well to prevent raveling.
Bullion Fringe	A long, twist-looped fringe. The top is permanently stitched. Used for upholstery, ottomans, window treatments.	Length: 3"–8"	Zipper foot	See cord-edge corner sewing (page 10). Hand miter corners for top application (G); do not clip.	Butt ends; do not overlap (F).	See loop fringe (above). Untwist plies to use as matching cord trim.

G

Hand miter corners

Working with Decorative Trims

Trim Type	Description	Size	Tools Required	Corner Sewing	Finishing	Tips
Tassel Fringe	A trim with many small tassels hanging from a flat gimp edge. Gimp is inserted into a seam or stitched on top of project.	Length: 2", including gimp edge	Zipper foot	See bullion fringe (page 11), for insertion or top application.	Turn cut edge under ½". Overlap ends ½" (J). Stitch.	Combine with other trims to layer for added texture.
Braid (Gimp)	Narrow, flat trim used to cover upholstery tacks or to edge pillow panels, cornices.	Width: ⅜"–⅝"	Flat presser foot	Top application only (H); hand miter corners (I).	Fold cut end under ½". Overlap ends by ½" (J).	Pin well to avoid uneven stitching.
Piping (Welting)	Cord wrapped with bias fabric. Used to edge and strengthen sewn seams. Purchase ready-made or make your own. (See "Making Welting" on page 13 for instructions on how to make your own welting.)	Diameter: 5⁄32", ½"	Zipper foot	Stitch along casing stitching; stop 1" before corner. Clip at corner, then stitch to corner; pivot with needle in fabric. Push corner trim away from you; lower foot and continue stitching.	Overlap ends 1". Clip and remove casing stitches from one end. Open casing; clip inside cords to butt (K). Fold open casing under ½", then wrap casing around joint (L). Stitch to close (M).	The amount of trim should match the amount of fabric. Do not pull trim. When in doubt, ease trim into place.

H Stitch along each edge

I Hand miter corners

J To finish: fold end under ½"; overlap cut ends ½"

K Clip inside cord — Clip corners

L Fold casing under ½". Wrap joint

M Stitch to close

Making Welting

Welting, also known as piping, is available ready-made by the yard or can be made with a strip of bias-cut fabric wrapped around a filler cord. The filler cord, available in various diameters at notions counters, is best when it is constructed of a net-covered cotton cord rather than of twisted multi-ply cable cord. The most popular diameters are $5/32$" or $1/4$", but a fatter cord will add emphasis on pillows and on round table covers.

To construct welting, take a rectangle of fabric and fold it diagonally, aligning the crosswise grainline to the lengthwise grainline to find the true bias (A).

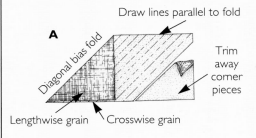

A — Diagonal bias fold — Draw lines parallel to fold — Trim away corner pieces — Lengthwise grain — Crosswise grain

Then cut fabric strips parallel to this fold line and piece them together to achieve the required length. To determine the width of the fabric strips, multiply the cord diameter by 3, then add 1" (for a $1/4$" cord, for example, you would need strips measuring $1/4$" times 3 plus 1", or $1\frac{3}{4}$" wide). Mark as many parallel lines as necessary, this same distance apart, so the total length exceeds the required amount of welting.

For a short total length, cut and stitch the pieces individually, right sides together, along the straight grainline short ends. For a longer piece of welting, create a continuous pieced strip as follows: on the marked piece of fabric, join the short strip ends, right sides together, so one strip extends unconnected at each side (B).

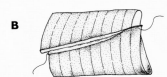

B

Stitch a $1/4$" seam; press it open. Starting at one of the extended edges, cut along the marked line across the stitched seam, creating one continuous piece of joined bias fabric (C).

C — Cut on lines

Place the bias strip wrong side up. With the filler cord at the center, fold the bias strip over the cord, aligning the long cut fabric edges. Use the zipper foot to stitch through both layers of fabric, using a medium to long stitch length. Stitch as close to the encased cord as possible.

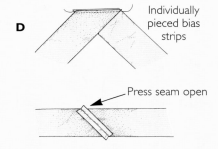

D — Individually pieced bias strips — Press seam open

Tassels

One exquisite tassel can impact an entire room. The largest tassels are usually seen attached to a cord tieback, hanging gracefully from pulled-back window treatments. While expensive, their layered, multicolored designs create dramatic appeal whether swinging from pillars and plant stands or wrapped around pillows and bathroom towels. Large cluster tassels and key tassels are often displayed individually to adorn a drawer pull or antique key (hence the name key tassel). Small, delicate tassels can be scattered on pillows, boxes, picture frames, and other accessories for interesting detail.

Tassels are commonly available in sizes from 2" to 8" long. Some tassels have only a small top loop for attachment and must be hand stitched or glued into place. The top loop is sometimes adjustable; if it does slide, be sure to add a stitch or a drop of glue to secure it to your project. The longer 3" loop on many medium-size tassels can be machine stitched easily into the corners of a pillow or table cover. The table "Working with Tassels" (page 14) describes the different types of tassels available and how to work with them. You can also make tassels of your own design; refer to the instructions on the next four pages.

Working with Tassels

Type	Uses	Size	Application
Small	Used for pillows, jewelry boxes, table covers, hats, dolls.	2"–3" long, ¼"–½" wide, with ½" loop	Hand sew or hot-glue.
Medium	Used for pillow corners, shade pulls, table covers, boxes.	3"–4" long, ½" wide, with 3" loop	Use zipper foot at corners.
Long Key Tassel	Used for pillow accents, shade pulls, table covers.	4"–6" long, ½"–¾" wide, with ½"–1" loop	Hand sew, hot-glue, or use zipper foot to machine sew.
Cluster Tassel	Used on antique keys, drawer pulls, lamp pulls, pillow accents.	3"–4" long, 3"–4" wide	Hand sew, hot-glue, or tie.
Festoon Tassel	Large tassel with opening at top to insert a cord. Used as a tasseled cord.	6"–8" long, 3" wide, with ½" opening at top	Hot-glue a cord into the top for hanging or tying.

Trim and Tassel Projects
~

Simple Wrap-and-Tie Tassel

1. Wrap yarn or embroidery floss around a piece of cardboard cut to the desired length of the finished tassel (A). Wrap 15–20 times for a slim tassel, 25–30 times for a tassel of medium thickness, or 30–50 times for a large tassel. Add or subtract wraps to adjust thickness. Mix yarns for interest.

2. Cut a 12" length of yarn. Fold it in half and knot it 3" from the fold, forming a 3" loop with two 3" tails. Slip one tail under the wrapped yarns (B), then tie snugly so that the loop is on the outside and the knotted ends are under the wrapped yarns. Slide the cardboard out from under the wrapping (C), leaving looped yarns tied securely at the top.

3. To wrap the top of the tassel, cut a 36" length of yarn. Place the yarn against the top of the tassel so that one end hangs to the bottom tassel edge. Form a small loop at the tassel top with the remaining yarn (D). Hold the loop and end in place with one hand and wrap the remaining yarn snugly around the tassel head ½" from the top. Work toward the top of the tassel until about ¼"–½" is covered and the loop protrudes above the wrapping. Insert the end of the wrapping yarn through the loop (E). Pull the other end of the wrapping yarn down (F), drawing the loop under the wrapped yarn.

4. Clip through the bottom tassel loops; trim the ends as necessary to even.

Wrap-and-Tie Tassel

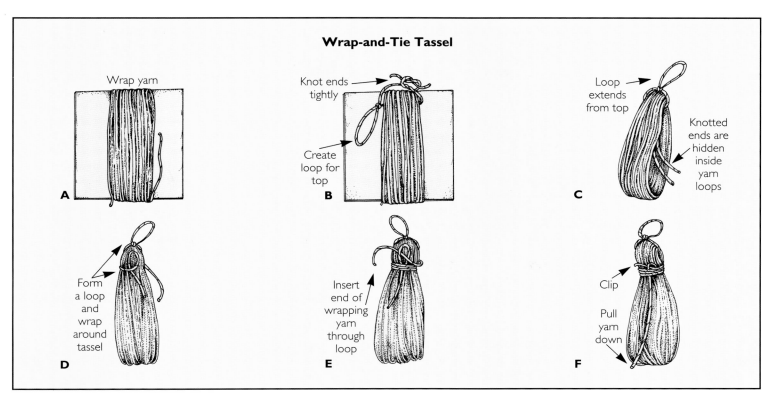

Wrap yarn

A

Form a loop and wrap around tassel

D

Knot ends tightly

Create loop for top

B

Insert end of wrapping yarn through loop

E

Loop extends from top

Knotted ends are hidden inside yarn loops

C

Clip

Pull yarn down

F

Coil-and-Glue Tassel

Materials

27" length of twisted cord, ³⁄₁₆" diameter

³⁄₈–½ yard of fringe, 3–6" long

Hot-glue gun and glue sticks

1. Glue one cut and taped cord end onto the top fringe edge, ¼" in from one side (A).

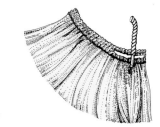

A

Apply a 1" bead of glue along the top fringe edge, then roll the fringe, sandwiching the cord

end in the fringe. Continue to glue and roll the fringe, working with 2" sections (B).

B

2. Form a ½" loop with the cord at the tassel top. Glue the cord down along the top side edge of the tassel. Wind the cord around the tassel at the top of the fringes, gluing the cord in place as you work (C).

C

Wind toward the top so that each coil of cord touches the one before. Use glue sparingly to prevent oozing.

3. As you reach the top, wrap the remaining cord (use no glue) to determine the cord length required to finish. Wrap a length of tape around the cord at the desired point and cut through the tape to remove the excess cord. Wrap and glue the remaining cord around the tassel loop. Push the taped cord end into the tassel center with the point of a scissor to conceal (D). (*Tip:* Cut the taped end to ⅛" so a minimum of tape remains.)

D

Tasseled Tieback

Choose your own fringe, cords, and color combination to create a dazzling tasseled tieback at one-third the cost of imported tiebacks. This tassel will hang from looped cords that are approximately 16" long. Add 4" of cord for every 1" of additional finished length required. Tassel fringe can be added to this tassel before the cord is wrapped for added interest. For a dramatic tassel, use bullion fringe. The bullion fringe can also be untwisted to created a matching cord for the tassel top wrap.

Materials

2½ yards of twisted cord, ⅜"–½" diameter

¾ yard of fringe, 3"–4" long

1½ yards of twisted cord, ³⁄₁₆" diameter

Hot-glue gun and glue sticks

1. *Tieback:* holding the larger twisted cord in your left hand, form a 16" loop, starting 4½" from one cut end. Wrap the long cord end 4 times around the base of the loop, at the 4½" point (A), working from left to right—actually wrapping the cord around your thumb. (Do not remove your left thumb from the looped knot until instructed to do so.)

A

With your right hand, pass the cord end back through the 4 wraps, right to left and out the left side (B).

B

Curl the working cord end around the 4½" end and pass it back through the 4 loops (C).

C

Remove your thumb; slowly pull the loops to adjust the length (D). The cut ends should remain about 4" long (E).

D

E

If the cut ends are uneven, you can untie and try again, or you can wrap with tape and trim evenly.

2. *Tassel:* cut the fringe and the ³⁄₁₆"-diameter cord each into 2 equal pieces (be sure to tape the cord first). Place one 4" end of the tieback over the top fringe edge. Glue and roll (F) as in Step 1 of "Coil-and-Glue Tassel" (page 15). Repeat for the second tieback end and the remaining fringe.

F

3. To wrap the top of each tassel, place one cord end at the top fringe edge, with the taped end pointing up. Glue and wrap the cord around the tassel (G), covering the starting end and working from the bottom to the top.

G

At the tassel top, finish as in Step 3 of "Coil-and-Glue Tassel" (page 15) (H). Repeat for the second tassel.

H

Working with Tiebacks

Type	Uses	Size	Application
Tasseled Tieback 	Large single or double tassel attached to looped cords. Used to pull back draperies.	6"–8" long tassels on a looped cord that measures approximately 30" from loop to loop	Tie onto or around project. No sewing required.
Cord Tieback	Thick twisted cord used to pull back draperies.	1" diameter, approximately 30" from end to end	Hang from end loops to wall hooks. No sewing required.

For the next project, keep in mind that ½" seams are allowed. When applying trims, refer to the tables "Working with Decorative Trims" (pages 10–12), and "Working with Tassels" (page 14). Start to sew all trims at the center of a side (choose the side that will be the least visible); never start at a corner. Ease the trim into place; never pull. The trimming should lie flat, with no puckers. If you choose to sew more than one row of trim, stitch each one separately, one at a time, on the ½" seam line.

Square Table Topper

A fringed square of fabric can be many things. Drape it over a round table by itself as a short tablecloth or over a fabric skirted table as a topper. Place it diagonally over a square table for a casual cover—or fashion your square from a soft challis fabric for an elegant shawl.

Materials

Fabric: Measure the table diameter. Decide how far you would like your topper to drop from each side. Table diameter + 2 × drop height = length (and width) of fabric square you will need.

Bullion fringe, 6" long: Measure the perimeter of the fabric square. Add ⅛ yard for ease and handling.

Matching thread

1. Finish all edges of the fabric square with a zigzag or overlock stitch.

2. Place the wrong side of the bullion fringe overlapping the right side of the fabric edge by ½" so that the fringes hang away from the fabric. Beginning at the center of one side, stitch the fringe in place (A).

A

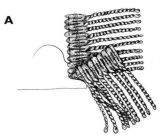

At each corner, hand fold the fringe into a neat miter; do not clip (B).

B

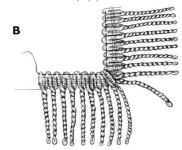

To finish the topper, cut the fringe ends cleanly, butt ends together, and stitch well to prevent raveling.

~

PART ONE

Living Spaces

Finishing details such as decorative trims and tassels can help to define a room's personality by highlighting and coordinating other furnishings. Sometimes a single clustered tassel, displayed like a piece of fine jewelry on a drawer pull or an antique key, is the only trim required to accessorize an entire room. More often, however, repeated or layered trims are necessary to link unlike colors or elements of design, such as an outlined pillow and chaise.

In each of the following photographs, the trim is integral to the decor—outlining, highlighting, emphasizing, and pulling otherwise disparate furniture pieces into unified harmony. An added border of lush fringe or simple pillows detailed with jaunty tassels may be the pièce de résistance for your own family room. Velvety fringe and silken cords can make the largeness of the great room more intimate. Color combinations created by layering tassel fringes of different colors can revitalize your entire living space. Walk through these beautifully decorated rooms and become inspired to embellish your own environment and transform your home into an enchanting, personalized living space.

Whether your home is centuries old, or a new, creatively designed living space, there is one room that receives the most attention—the living room, family room, or great room. It is the gathering place for the family—the area of every home that is the most "lived-in," bursting with warmth and life. Many homes have a family room and a living room, with the living room designed as a more formal space for show and entertaining. The family room, usually situated off the kitchen or dining area, rollicks with children and family activity. The great room combines both of these environments to create a large gathering area which becomes the heart of the home.

~

Opposite: In this intelligent and casual arrangement, botanical prints complement natural textures and colors. A collection of intriguing pillows in different shapes share a similar design scheme. Each pillow panel is flanked by shirred borders in cream, sage, and taupe, then edged in fluffy fringe. Cord-edge can be inserted between panels for added dimension, or added to the outer edge.

19

~

~

Left: Just one row of trimming can create texture and diversity as the multiple pillows in this simple monochromatic setting show. The overall sameness creates an environment of tranquillity. There are no surprises—just welcoming comfort.

Opposite: To lie in the lap of luxury—amid walls of distressed plaster and brick? Of course! These far from perfect walls are the ideal backdrop for luxurious furnishings in subdued tones of cream, rose, and sage green. Amassed pillows wrapped, gathered, and edged in sumptuous fringes and tassels create an atmosphere of casual elegance.

Below: This sofa, slipcovered in prewashed damask, evokes memories of summer at the lake and Grandma's screened-in porch, of faded cushions and fading childhood memories. An elaborate tassel-fringed pillow in a muted floral print enhances this nostalgic ambience. Nestled between its plainer cousins, it stands out like a cherished collectible book.

Above: Three comfy oversize chairs make an inviting seating arrangement in front of a cozy fireplace. The overstuffed pillows, with their looped ribbon fringe, seem poised for witty repartee. This whimsical, floppy fringe, constructed of looped seam binding, adds a cheerful, lighthearted edge to basic square pillows. Contrasting welt on the oversize chair with ottoman tames the grand scale of the furnishings.

~

Above: This room has no surprises; it is divided equally, each side a mirror image of the other. Because the outside land-scape is very important to the owner, draperies have been completely drawn so that nothing separates the room from the outdoors. The furniture is large in scale, but size is minimized by outlining the knife-edged cushions in caramel-colored welting to match the carpet. The tablecover flounce skimming the floor is also trimmed in this rich earthy tone. The room's natural palette allows the lush greenery viewed through the surrounding windows to dominate the scene.

~

Below: With patterned sky blue wallpaper above and a timeworn earthy brown floor below, this lovely corner imparts the feel of a Victorian park. The comfortable chair is dressed to impress, with full skirt draped to softly puddle onto the floor, and its midsection tied up with brown ribbons and bows. Pillows rest like fringe-trimmed shawls on the chair cushion. The wispy lace curtain is pulled aside with softly trailing potted ivy to view the garden beyond. Trim is kept to a minimum, in soft browns and naturals, repeating the double banding of the wall molding and the lower shadows of the windowsill.

23

~

Above: Casual slipcovering keeps furniture fresh in this living area. Pillows constructed of rich tapestry and brocade, framed in natural-colored fringe, balance the strong colors of the carpet below. White fringes edge a cool blue scarf valance that seems to glow in midday light.

ℒℯ𝒻𝓉: *Two-toned cord and bullion fringe accentuate the design of an exquisitely tufted ottoman while reflecting the green surround and rich wood of the fireplace. The rich textures and Floridian shades of coral and turquoise green enhance the high style of this 1930s-inspired room. Pillows on the sofa and chair are edged in trims that accent the tropical colors.*

ℒℯ𝒻𝓉: *This no-clutter, no-fuss interior holds very little to obscure the ocean view. Richly colored, sparsely trimmed pillows reflect this simple serenity.*

Left: Welting, carefully applied to match the fabric stripes, outlines this oversize chair and ottoman, giving shape to their oversize structures. Bullion fringe adds dimension to the small pillows, enabling them to equal the stature of the larger-scale furnishings. Layering tassel fringe with bullion fringe on the smallest pillow gives it added importance. Pillows are displayed according to size, with the less decorative designs in the back.

25

Opposite: This fringed, dusky mauve sofa is reminiscent of the 1940s. Soft fringes blend into the fabric like faded memories, offering a sense of security and warmth. Velvet pillows embellished with monochromatic fringes add to the ambience created with framed prints and period furnishings.

Below: Because trims work so well to integrate different elements of a room setting, one trim may not be enough to complete your decor. Color coordination is essential when using an assortment of decorative trims. Choose two or three companion styles to combine and interchange for depth and impact. Here, striped twisted cords end in full blue tassels, coordinating the brush fringe and enhancing the fabric coloration. The gold detail focuses the eye on the shape of the tassel as well as the item it adorns.

Above: The printed fabric in this window treatment displays a rather delicate motif, which is enhanced nicely by the lacelike tassel fringe suspended from its edges. The pale yellow valance, trimmed in tiny teardrop tassels, maintains continuity of color—it's as if the wall itself swagged gracefully across the window. The trimmings on the sofa and pillows echo the pale yellow color scheme.

Opposite: This great room has been divided into casual conversational and eating areas. Color and lighting remain constant throughout, binding the areas together. Fabric is draped across tall, cool brick walls, adding warmth and intimacy; lights have been dropped to achieve the same. Pillows, edged in fringe and plumped to exaggerate their full dimensions, complete the friendly ambience.

Below: Beneath a gilt-edged cloud of window fabric, a single velvet chair, tufted and trimmed with bullion fringe, sits like a throne. A Victorian pillow graces the velvet like a large cameo brooch. Candle sconces hang from cords ready to shed light into this somewhat primitive yet opulent room.

Above: Lush velvet sofas, silk fringe—swagged windows, deeply tufted ottomans—each of these flawlessly appointed furnishings begs to be touched. Fringed pillows and cord-trimmed sofa cushions complete this room's air of old world elegance and comfort.

Right: Red, black, and green fringe cascades to the floor, successfully extending this plaid table cover to a ruffly, splayed edge. Much more understated than the gilt-edged furniture and frames around it, this piece perfectly achieves the desired effect—displaying the fabric and its coloration to its best advantage.

30

Below: With a fringe-trimmed lamp above and tassel-trimmed table below, this glittering display glows with an opulent presence. The square topper is simple in construction but elaborate in detail. Impressive rosette tassels and cord decorate the edges like jewels on a evening gown, highlighting the gilt-edged tapestry as well as the gold-trimmed collection it displays.

Above: Lampshade and lamp are decorated with birds perched on fragile springtime branches. Tassel fringe, dangling from the shade edge, replicates the blossoms on the branches themselves, repeating the important, if subtle, design details.

Left: A strong influence of red and white is a welcome diversion in this dark, book-lined room. The unusual red patterned ottoman takes center stage in an intimate, conversational setting. Dark welting and bullion fringe emphasize the ottoman's unique curved lines as well as repeat the dark outline used on the tab-top drapes. Sofa pillows continue the color scheme with lush red fringe. Small details such as outlining and button tufting become important decorating themes when they are repeated throughout the room.

Right: Tassels can be attached to the ends of narrow twisted cord to create a "chair tie," designed to secure a seat cushion to a chair. Because this particular chair requires no such fastener, the red and tan ties are left to dangle on the arms as adornment, highlighting other red accents around the room. Other tasseled cords, fashioned in a natural color, serve as drapery tiebacks, retaining a lightness in the dark-patterned room.

Left: The shape of one window is echoed throughout this delightful room—in fabric motifs, chair caning, and a valance shape that mimics the arched design. East Indian splendor is reflected in brass accessories and tassels that sway from valance points. Simple chair ties secure chair cushions and create light-hearted movement.

33

Opposite: In this intimate seating area, pillows are lined up for inspection, each with its own unique edging or button detail. The pillows vary in color but fringes are all in natural tones to provide unity. The pillows' similar size ensures that no pillow will over-power another.

Above: A stone wall and carved fireplace mantel immediately set the tone of this charismatic room. Surface details on plump fringed throw pillows stand out in relief, demonstrating that texture need not be provided only by wood or stone. Even the smooth table surface has been casually draped with a fringed scarf, increasing the tactile possibilities. The invitation to sit and share an impromptu snack with friends is simply irresistible.

Left: With its floral bouquet of colors and a bay window alcove infused with sunshine yellow, this room is ideally suited for dining or entertaining. The red accents are of the same value as the yellow and balance perfectly when tied together by the crisp red welted pillows. The scalloplike shapes of the tassel-fringed valances show up distinctly against the well-lit windows, adding a subtle pink accent to pull all the pieces together.

Right: Color is the key here, as each trim style is coordinated down to individual threads. Finely threaded brush fringe, jacquard braid, a long silky tasseled tieback, and textured fringe are juxtaposed on vivid yellows and blues, displaying the ultimate in color coordination.

Above: Traditional furnishings take on new airs when transformed by this magnificent Moroccan-influenced window. Saturated colors permeate the room as the Moroccan flavor influences everything from a floor-skimming table topper to the bullion-fringed ottoman.

~

Opposite: These are
cheeky, self-important pillows.
The black and white self-made
welting on the colored pillows
coordinates the adjacent pillows in striking visual harmony.

~

Above: A true sense of humor is required to group these elements.
Vintage fabric pillows were given a shaggy edge of bullion fringe
to contrast the geometric lines of this retro living area. On the sofa, small
checked welting—chosen carefully in colors that enhance the pillows
and wall color alike—offers camaraderie to the checked fireplace.

Opposite: A stairway connecting sections of the house need not be steeped in anonymity. Drenched in a sunny yellow, this striking staircase begs to be seen. Navy drapes stand full length at the windows, swagged with long matching fringe to subtly break their overpowering height. In keeping with the golden floor of the landing, the petite bench is clothed in patterned gold satin with small matching tassels flowing from each bolster.

Below: In this display, each design element stands out in stark simplicity. The lines cannot be improved upon. In this uncluttered setting, the key tassel adornment dangles in singular beauty.

Above: Gold pyramids on a dramatic room screen seem suspended in midair. On the sofa, a square pillow is wrapped and edged with cord like a gift waiting to be opened. Twisted cord defines the oblong shape of a satin, multipatterned pillow.

Left: In such an ornate room, little added detail is required. The richly colored tapestry of the chair and ottoman is heightened by the blush-colored edging of the oblong pillow. The fringes, which match the tapestry flowers perfectly, become like flower petals themselves, framing the pillow and preventing the matching fabric from blending into obscurity.

42

Right: No edge is left untrimmed in this charming cottage-influenced room. Duo-toned trim is the subtle theme here: red and green fringe edges drapes and pillows; candy-striped cord-edge whips up pillow and chair edges to a frothy perfection. The heavy bullion-fringed lower sofa panel separates slightly different shades of white while echoing the dark table and carpet leaves. A change of tables and lamps takes this room from cottage decor to traditional. With the heavier influence of a dark floral carpet, the room grows warmer and more subdued, perfect for a change of season. The single gold tassel adorning the end table drawer is in tune with the increased formality, reflecting other brass-trimmed accessories.

43
~

~

Above: Myriad colors and styles combine in this room to demonstrate the best in eclectic decorating.
Prints of different scales balance each other with bands of solid red, with trim kept to a minimum. Functional gimp,
designed to cover upholstery tacks, finishes chairs while simple cord-edge adds structural shape to the oversize sofa pillows.
The surface texture of the red rosettes adorning the windows seems to be repeated in the red scroll slipper chairs
as well as in the more subtle blue textural pattern on the love seat.

Dining Possibilities

The dining area is more than a place to eat. As a showroom of inviting decor and exquisite furniture, it serves to gather friends together for conversation and the camaraderie shared during the presentation of a fine meal. But even without a roomful of guests, the dining room, with its highly polished table and gleaming table accessories, can be the dressiest room in the home. Since it often shares space with, or can be viewed from, the great room, the dining room may contain elements of larger decorating themes. Such a flow of colors and styles creates a cohesive decorated environment.

Decorative trims, used elsewhere to highlight a color or theme, can be repeated in the dining area. Because of the small size of utensils and details inherent in table place settings, scale is more critical in the dining room than in other areas of the home. Sometimes a narrower version of a large trim used elsewhere is ideal for edging table runners, place mats, or napkins. The companion trim, such as brush or bullion fringe, is then used to finish the tablecloth hem or coordinating window treatment, carrying the color and textural theme throughout the room. Cords ending in colorful tassels may be designed to secure a seat cushion to the chair, but they also have surprising impact when used to tie up a creative napkin arrangement!

For special occasions and holidays, the addition of new table toppers or place mats can instantly change the feel of the room. Whatever the occasion, whether the table is set for a formal affair or a casual repast with friends, dining decor should remain exciting and inviting, while retaining a unity with adjacent rooms. Small details such as decorative embellishment can achieve this continuity while creating everyday appeal in an ever-changing, well-dressed dining room.

Opposite: No dinner is planned, but this rooms shines with an air of expectancy. To allow the sunshine to enter, the dramatic draperies are pulled to the side with large, multicolored tasseled tiebacks. Because they match the fabric so well, they maintain an unbroken expanse of color from floor to ceiling. The scallop motif, repeated throughout the room, is first seen in the decorative edging, silhouetted along the drapes' leading edge. Larger scallops are featured in the double swagged valance, which is mounted at the ceiling to call attention to an antique gold border with a subtle, echoing pattern.

Left: These deeply pleated plaid shades are a perfect liaison between the rustic beamed ceiling and the ornate Asian carpet. The thick weighted cotton fringe reinforces the natural toned detail in the carpet and the light shade of the walls, adding a casual note to an otherwise formal dining room.

45

46
~

~

Above: This charming display of multiple patterns is unified by colors of the same value on different furnishings. Sheer white drapes are tied high, then fall freely to the floor, maintaining the sense of height created by the outer drapes. The blue patterned welt, which edges the custom padded cornice, and the red and blue decorative trim coordinate the drapery fabric, while the window tiebacks and tablecloth bring a nice sense of balance to the room. The decorative edging also serves to keep the eye inside the room, instead of gazing outward to the vista beyond.

~

Right: The small beaded fringe which edges this striped valance incorporates just the novelty necessary to combine such diverse prints. The ultimate result is a room ripe with wit and eclectic appeal.

~

Below: This delightful pantry brings elements that might otherwise be hidden in a cupboard into plain view. The fanciful character of these displayed vegetables and antique utensils glows with the light reflected off yellow walls. Lace doilies and Battenburg hangings edge shelves to lend an air of country charm. The trim on the yellow valance is subtle, but enhances the old-fashioned ambience of the area.

Right: Many details delight the eye in this dramatic dining area. Large tassels prevail, with silvery swagged valances pulled high at the corners to allow the edges to fall into soft triangles at the corners. This triangular shape mimics that of the large tassels that pull aside the elegant green draperies. To complete this festive theme, a tablecloth covered with a tassel pattern has been chosen for the large round table.

48

Left: A table, which might otherwise hold potted plants and collectibles, has been cleared and set for a light luncheon. Decorative trims in shades of tea and coffee have been selected to edge the table topper, slipcover, and pillow, creating a natural, earthy feel for this quiet sitting room.

Opposite: In this intimate dining area, a bullion-fringed table cover picks up the creamy tones of the draperies. The blue and white drapery edging seems an extension from the fabric itself, creating a border which is at once elaborate and comfortable. Self-covered welt used to reinforce the chair cushion edges allows the pattern to remain unimpeded by the seams.

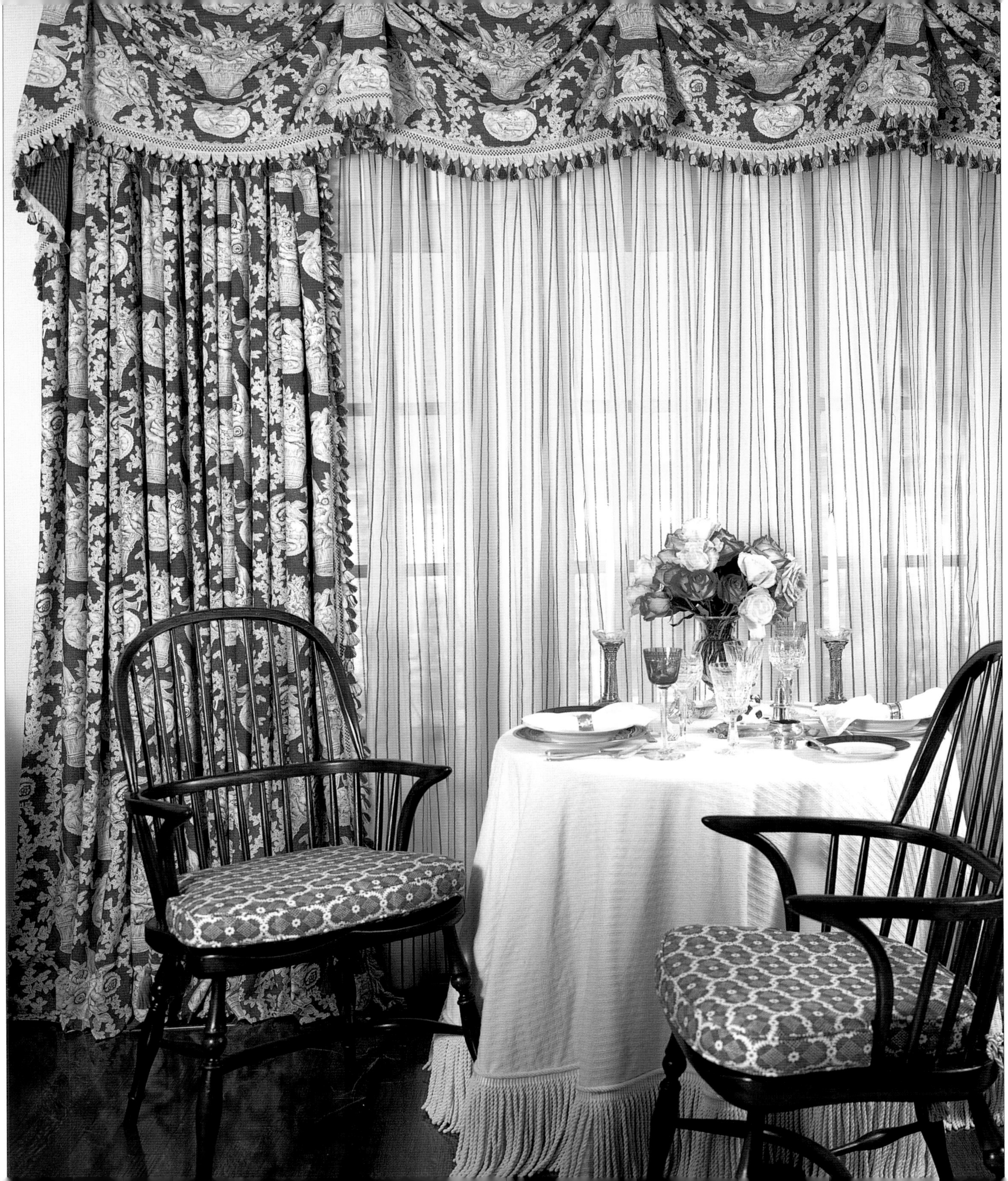

~

Bed and Bath

The bedroom and bathroom are the most personal rooms in the home; their environments must please no one but you. As the room which represents the ultimate in comfort and luxury, the bedroom is ideally suited for lavish trims and embellishment. Fringes and tassels are perfect to edge bed coverings and window treatments or to accent collectibles, while trims and silky braids can adorn pillows and antique boxes.

Styles can vary dramatically. Embellishment can range from lavishly layered tassel fringe to pristine Battenburg laces to a single lush tassel. Trims may be inserted into the seams of home-sewn decor, or can be added to existing bed coverings. For example, the addition of bullion fringe to the edge of a coverlet can transform a plain square of fabric into a sumptuous bed covering. You can edge a comforter and matching bed shams with a row of welting to add color, or pile small bed pillows—each with different embellished surface detail—high on a bed or window seat to add depth and personality.

A home office often competes for important bedroom space, but it need not diminish the design appeal. By borrowing elements from elsewhere in the room, you can integrate these furnishings, actually improving the intrinsic design value of the room. A beautiful tassel, dangling from a desk drawer, can repeat and reflect room color schemes, and at the same time soften the hard edges of the office corner.

Whether the private rooms in your home serve as functional work spaces or quiet retreats, the beautiful photographs on the pages that follow will inspire you to create your own intimate design environment.

~

Opposite: Amid finely striated marble walls, a full, rich window shade edged in a profusion of tassel fringe creates dramatic focal impact. Pulled up into cascades of fabric and trim, the shade creates a graceful bottom line, not unlike the curves of the double mirrors.

~

Left: Shades of sand and ocean blues and greens transform this small bathroom into an underwater fantasy. Swaying ferns and mythical warriors clash on a camouflaged bathtub, filling this narrow room with movement and life. Blue stripes, added to make the room appear wider, further the illusion of a watery atmosphere. Twisted cords in shades of blue repeat these stripes on a cascading fabric skirt.

Opposite: This room is a testament to quiet elegance and refined taste. The owners have chosen the item they wish to stand out above all others— the striking curved bench placed at the foot of their bed. So that no other wood competes for attention, the bed frame was padded, tufted, and covered in fabric to match the bedspread. The height of the bedposts helps to keep the bench in proportion; sumptuous corded tassels tied to each post accentuate the color and satiny texture of the bed coverings without dominating the simplicity of the bench. The green fabric-covered walls reflect the softly striped fabric of the bench and balloon shades.

53

Above: A softly gathered valance crowns the windows in this spacious bedroom. Green edging on valance and drape edges adds height and defines each window's slender shape. It also serves to differentiate the pattern, which is repeated throughout the room. Often, fringe can be an integral part of construction as on the shawl thrown carelessly on the chaise. This lovely shawl could serve as a topper elsewhere in the room, adding texture and emphasis to the color scheme.

Left: Cherished childhood friends gaze out at a beribboned room from the comfort of the upholstered child-size chair. A rose-colored twisted cord embeds itself in the tufting of a larger green shell-back chair and continues into button-topped tassels. This same color of tasseled cord is used for tiebacks that blend with the busy drapery fabric design. The green welting on the ruffled window treatment not only allows the drape to stand out against the printed wallpaper, but helps to emphasize the architecturally inspired valance.

~

Above: A partial canopy transforms an awkward, chopped-up room into this inviting alcove. The tassel fringe edging the canopy is simply top-stitched to an already finished hem—an easy application technique for ready-made drapes or hemmed sheeting. Its rich, dark color intensifies the colors of the floor runner and the leaf-printed wallpaper. The wallpaper bands the room, lending a sense of continuity to uneven walls and keeping the eye focused on the inviting gold glow of the canopy.

Above: Multicolored tassel fringe draws its hues from this room's palette, blending dusty blue and gold into burnished harmony. The scalloped edge of the custom bed cover stands in contrast to the bed frame, softening the tailored lines and accentuating the fringe itself. (Multicolored tassel fringe can be purchased in combined colors, or it can be created by layering assorted solid-color trims.) The welting on the form-fitting bed cover mimics the gold in the wallpaper striping. Tone-on-tone draperies are edged in narrow fringe so perfectly matched it seems a part of the fabric itself. The drapes are pulled softly to the side with matching tasseled tiebacks so as not to break the natural vertical flow. Because the wall stripes and draperies are large in scale, the larger-than-life portrait over the bed surveys the room in perfect balance.

~

ℒeft: Soft curves in varying sizes link pieces of this bed-room corner together. A single swag curves gracefully above the mirror-topped dressing table. The buttercup yellow scallops serve as a backdrop to highlight the tassel-fringed edge of the swagged valance. The soft gray and white pattern of a slipcovered chair and skirted dressing table highlights the gilt scallop-edged plates mounted on the adjacent wall.

57

~

Left: A black wrought iron bed is plumped with down, then loosely wrapped in soft white cotton. A red bed skirt and pillow accents match the red draperies and add a festive air. The raffia and natural-colored tassels clustered on the bedpost, along with natural fringe and the fat, shirred welt of the table skirt hem, keep this soaring room earthbound.

$\mathcal{A}bove:$ These red clad windows admit just enough morning sun to reflect the satin sheen of hardwood floors and golden faux finished walls.

The down duvet is bundled at the foot of the bed and cinched with rich bronze passementerie.

~

Above: This cozy bedroom showcases family memorabilia, antiques, and crisp bed coverings reminiscent of heirloom linens. Stacked white pillows and a Battenburg draped headboard add Continental appeal. In keeping with the elegant simplicity, the antique bedside dresser is adorned with only a floppy key tassel.

~

Opposite: The treasures in this playfully nostalgic dressing room were chosen not only as mementos of childhood but for their black and white coloration. The walls and cabinet work are capped with a black and white striped canopy, edged in artfully scalloped binding that mimics the black-bordered rug. A photograph of exquisite stained glass hung from a tasseled cord is a charming way to enhance fabric behind it and offers a window to the past.

~

Below: A bed can be fully draped for reasons other than privacy and warmth. These bed drapes provide relief from the dark walls and draw the eye upward to the canopied ceiling. Tan fringe softens the stark whiteness of the drapes while effectively accentuating the warm golden tones of the box and bed side table accessories. The white bed contrasts dramatically with the rich, dark walls.

Opposite: This room is arranged to make the most of a cool breeze on a sultry summer day. The mirrored dressing table reflects the view through the large windows—windows meant not to enclose but to frame the surrounding picturesque countryside. The wrought iron bed offers a hint of structure in a white-on-white environment, while the tasseled bed curtains add just a touch of color—and a lot of elegance.

63

Above: Carefully chosen details make this a bedroom as delightful to enter as it is difficult to leave. Drapes, edged in satiny bullion fringe that just kisses the plank floor, are pulled aside to splash sunshine on the white furnishings. White hydrangeas spill over a sculpted white iron flower box; a vintage treasure box hides below. The shining brass bed, with its lace-trimmed coverlet, complements the room's rich textures and simple styling.

~

Above: The use of lavish fabric and fringe decor was taken a step further in this room by casting a dimensional valance from plaster. In true trompe l'oeil fashion, painted fringes and tassels are quite real in appearance, but with its cap of wings this vision becomes a true flight of fancy.

~

Opposite: An antique cape served as the source of design inspiration for this richly patterned room. Drapery trim was chosen because of its similarity to the border so artfully applied to the cape centuries ago, adding authenticity and character. Tasseled tiebacks draped low on the curtains are an unexpected and interesting touch.

Opposite: Walls and mirrors in this elegant bathroom have been covered with intricate painted designs duplicating the printed window fabric. The fabric itself, displayed only at the large casement window, is edged in a soft white scallop and pulled back with clean white tasseled ties.

Right: An older bathroom is rejuvenated with fabric-trimmed accessories. Shirred fabric encloses the lamp cord as well as the shower rod, while braided trim bands the pedestal sink and pulls back the lined shower curtain. Even the hard edges of the mirror are camouflaged in softly folded fabric. Coordinated monotonal fabric makes this fabric-themed room an easy-care, easy-on-the-eyes environment.

68

Opposite: Warm tones and a sense of serenity emanate from this restrained and sophisticated work area. The blending of old with new achieves a quiet peace where wooden boxes, cherished photos, and potted plants bring life to this corner hideaway. The single blue clustered key tassel lends an air of importance to the desk while drawing together the blue tones of the urn, the framed artwork, and the contemporary window shades.

Above: This unusual cane secretary was not meant to be tucked into a corner. Instead it receives proper attention here as the overseer to this room with a view. The lakeside window is framed with swagged and pleated draperies of a delicate floral print, edged in the softest pink and celadon scallops. The shaggy fringed pillow, added to ensure comfortable seating, is a reminder that this desk is not neglected. Hours spent here penning letters or updating a journal pass pleasantly with favorite figurines and prizewinning flowers nearby.

Sources

~

Materials and Supplies

Decorative trims and tassels as well as components to make your own are available at local fabric and craft stores and by mail. Consult a telephone directory to locate neighborhood sources, and check advertisements in craft, decorating, and sewing magazines for mail-order sources. Sewing fairs open to the public are good places to locate hard-to-find design materials and instructional books.

Spectacular trims and tassels normally available through "the trade only" may be sourced through interior designers or decorator outlets. Antique and vintage shops and flea markets are good places to locate unusual trims and tassels, too. Coordinating accessories, such as lace and pillows, can be found in fabric stores or in bed, bath, and home furnishing stores.

General sewing and craft supplies, such as scissors, needles, pins, glue, and sewing machines, are sold both at fabric stores and through many mass merchants.

Design Ideas

The myriad of home decorating magazines on the market offers a wide range of creative ideas. Visiting decorator showcases in your area is another way to review new design possibilities. Home furnishing mail-order catalogs have won-derful suggestions, too. Home sewing pattern companies offer patterns that are strikingly similar to a treatment you might like to try; with a little inspiration and modification, you can achieve the look you're after.

Save your favorite design concepts in an idea file for reference later; that way, you'll always have a little bit of inspiration on hand.

Reading

Consult a newsstand, fabric store, or public library for books and articles on trims and tassels. General decorating books and books that emphasize decorating with fabric also offer a multitude of ideas and tips. Listed below are some books that provide ideas and technical help beyond the scope of this book.

Dickens, Susan. *The Art of Tassel Making*. Kenthurst, New South Wales: Kangaroo Press, 1995.

Frankel, Candie. *Pillowmaking*. New York: Little, Brown, 1993.

Paine, Melanie. *New Fabric Magic*. New York: Random House, 1995.

————. *Fabric Magic*. New York: Pantheon Books, 1987.

Welch, Nancy. *Tassels: The Fanciful Embellishment*. Asheville, N.C.: Lark Books, 1992.

Conversion Chart for Common Measurements

~

The following chart lists the approximate metric equivalents of inch measurements up to 20", rounded for practical use. To calculate equivalents not listed, multiply the number of inches by 2.54cm. To convert 36", for example, multiply 36 times 2.54, for an equivalent of 91.44cm, or 91.5cm when rounded.

½" = 1.3cm	
1" = 2.5cm	11" = 28cm
2" = 5cm	12" = 30.5cm
3" = 7.5cm	13" = 33cm
4" = 10cm	14" = 35.5cm
5" = 12.5cm	15" = 38cm
6" = 15cm	16" = 40.5cm
7" = 18cm	17" = 43cm
8" = 20.5cm	18" = 45.5cm
9" = 23cm	19" = 48cm
10" = 25.5cm	20" = 51cm

Index

~

~

Photography Credits